Chronicles of Shade

Series by
Ken Kennett and Gérard Maillé

Chronicles of
Shade

As researched and narrated
by
Professor Olivia Owl

ISBN: 978-0-9942264-0-2

Born in Germany, Olivia Owl commenced her education in the Black Forest.

She continued her studies in the Landes Forest, France, the Hoia Baciu Forest, Romania, the Belovezhskaya Pushcha Forest, Belarus, the Trillemarka - Rollagsfjell Forest, Norway, and then in Washington's Colville National Forest, where she gained her Doctorate.

Olivia is now Research Professor of Sexology in England's Sherwood Forest.

PLEASE NOTE !!

The names of those involved in this and following case studies
have been changed in order to protect their privacy
and otherwise mostly unblemished reputations.

The Cat and the Canary

CASE STUDY NUMBER 1

It was a day *Candice* would never forget !

There she was, preparing herself for her daily recital.

Candice was a gifted singer,

and had chosen for her program that day a selection of
Operatic Arias.

She had just started her favourite Aria,
the "*Queen of The Night*" from *Mozart's* "*Magic Flute*",

when she was suddenly interrupted by an alluring **smell**,

which in no way could be attributed to *Timmy* !

Looking down from her perch, Candice was amazed to discover

the most **attractive** stranger imaginable !

However, what was a little disturbing

was the way *Christopher* was eyeing her...

...not in the way Timmy saw things,

but with a look of a different persuasion !

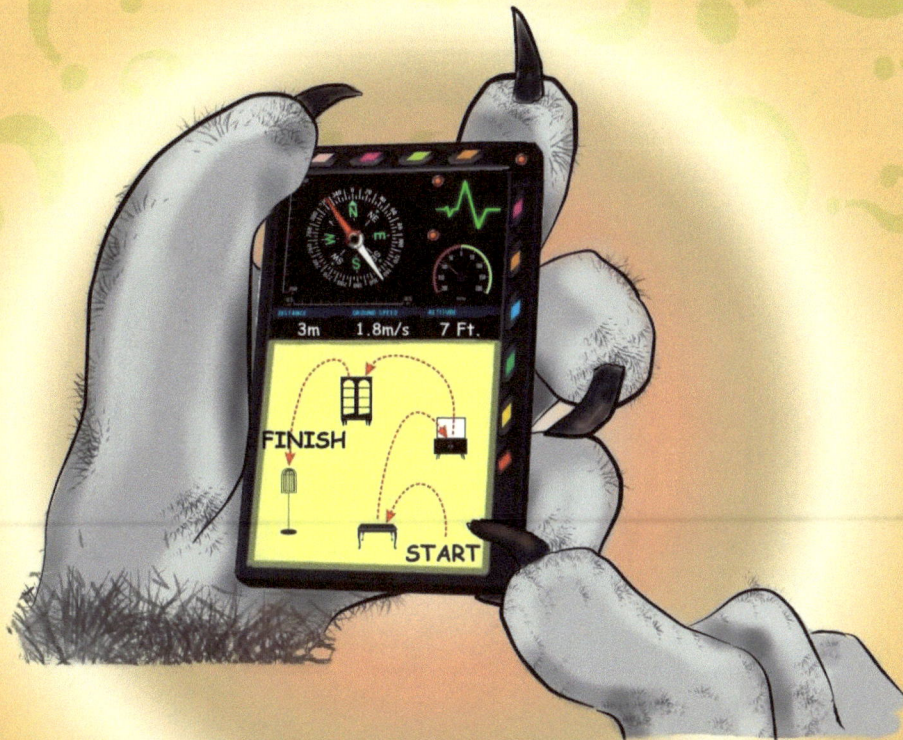

Before Candice knew it, Christopher had sprung to the coffee table,
from there to the TV stand, then to the china, glassware and trophy cabinet,
and finally, displaying remarkable athleticism,

arrived at his desired destination !

Instantly, Candice's world was turned on its head !

Seizing on the moment,

Christopher clawed his way to the top,

until he and Candice had come together as one, **feather to fur !**

Feather to Fur
1874 - 1875

For
Portrait details
see Appendix

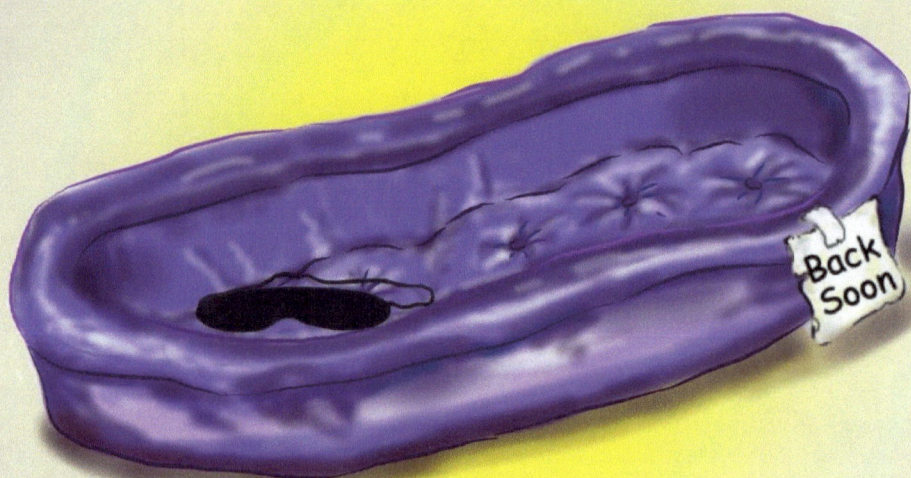

Where was Timmy when all this was happening?

What followed was an incident
that beggars all description,
but needless to say,
and indeed it needs to be said,

Candice lost her "composure",

not once, **not twice, but three times over !**

Mission accomplished, Christopher withdrew his support,

and Candice plummeted into the sea
of seed and water newly located on the bottom of her cage.

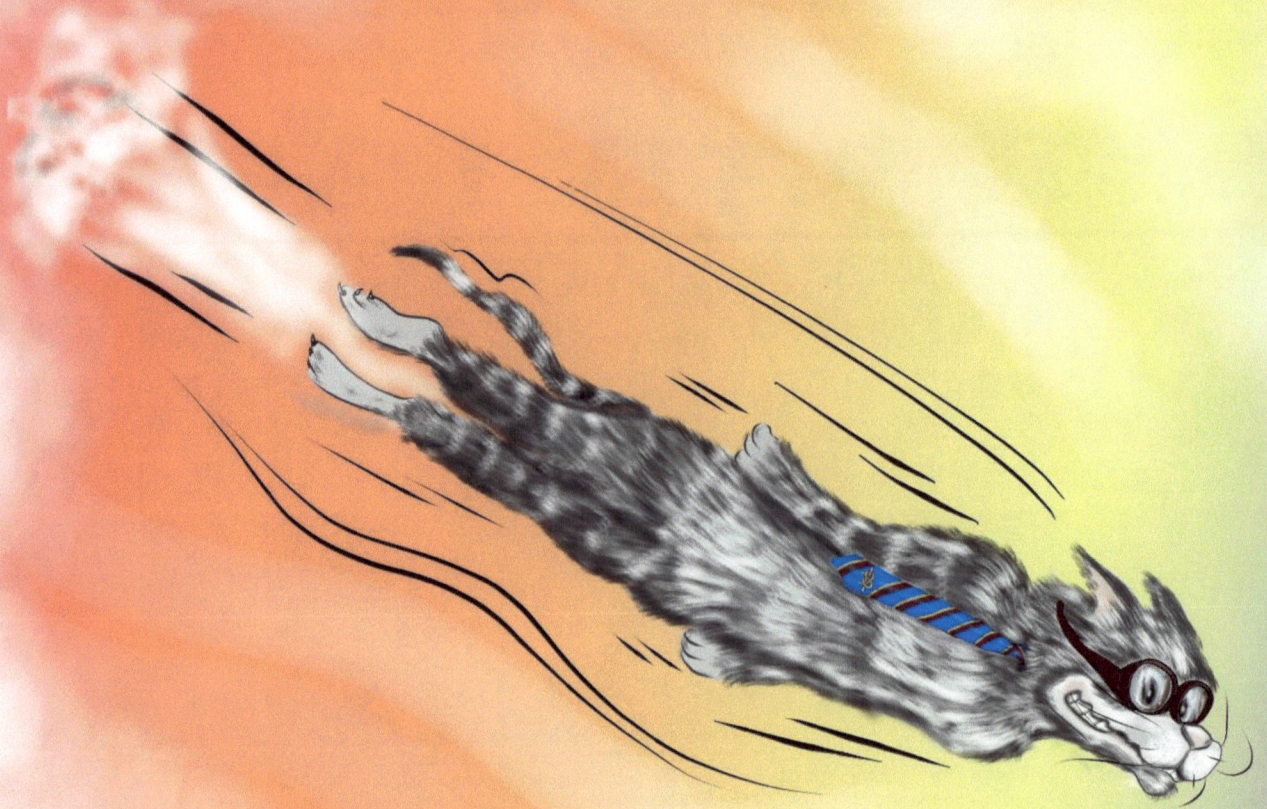

At the speed of sound, Christopher departed the scene...

...swaggering out of sight.

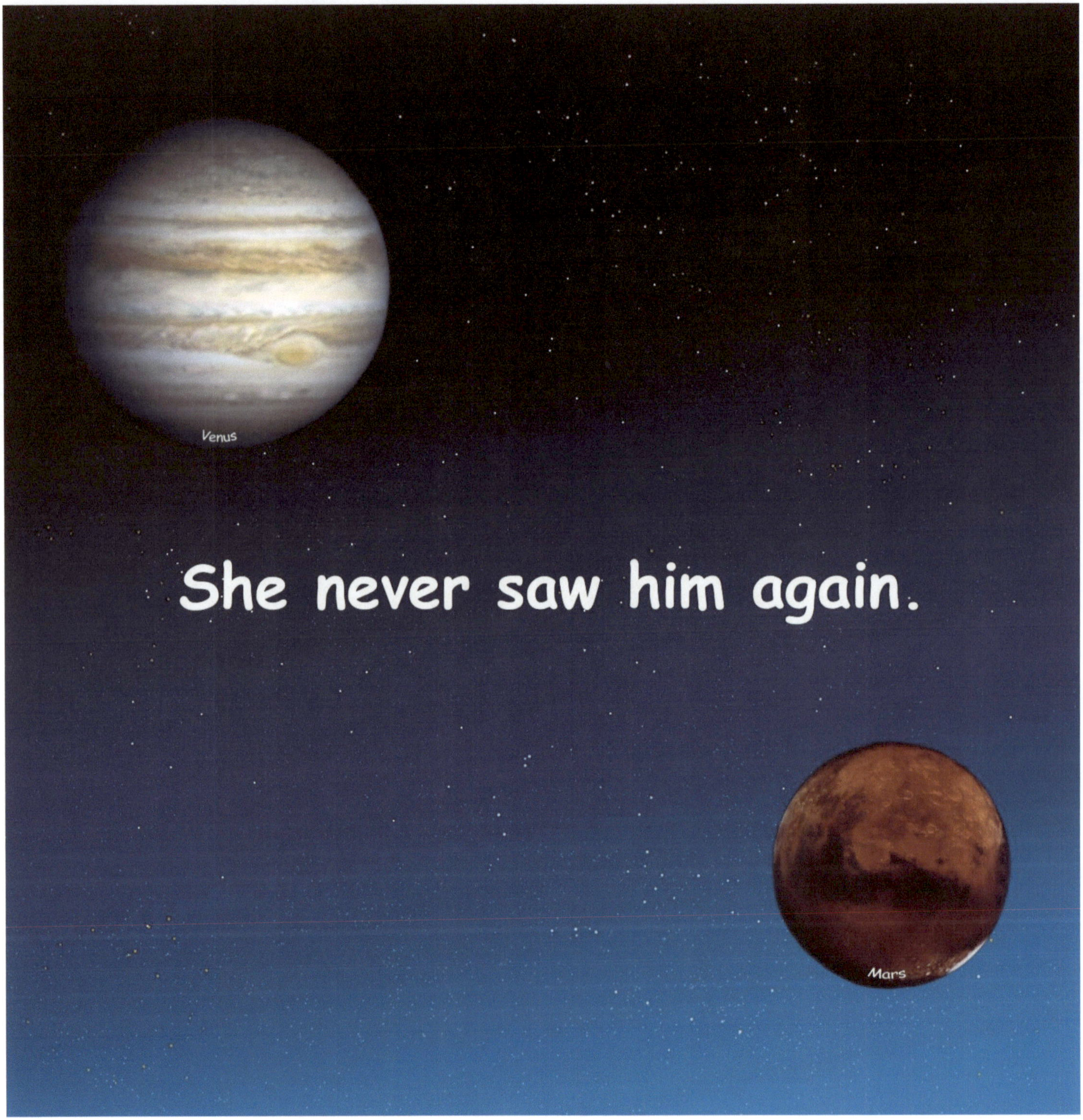
Venus
Mars

She never saw him again.

From that day on,
Candice only ever performed a *Blues* repertoire.

Scream Blue Murder
Blue Tit
Blue in the Face
Blue Wail
A Bolt from the Blue
Bluen Away

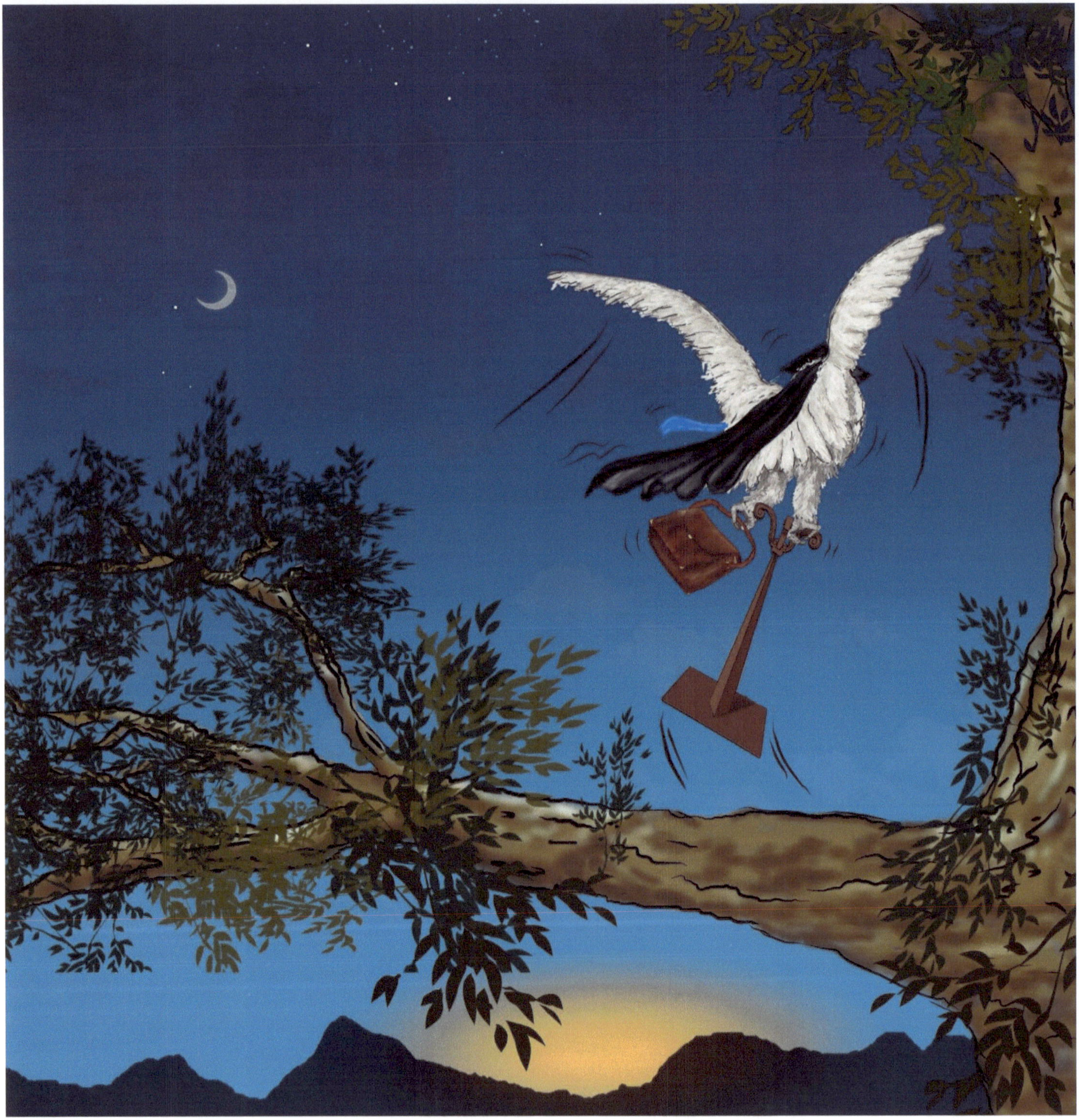

Professor Olivia Owl

Professor Owl enjoys a DOGGY *(Doctor of Gruelling Grunting Yelling)*,
a BANG *(Bondage and Nefarious Games)* and
is a SPANKA *(Sleazy Perversions and Nameless Kinky Activities)*.

She is also an authority on R'n'R *(Rubber and Rope)*
and is the recipient of a ROAR *(Repatriation of Aggrieved Roadies)*
for her services to the Music Industry.

Appendix

Feather to Fur [1874 - 1875]

Paletto Pubico   1853 -1937

One of the world's leading Impressionists, and founder of the *Pubic Movement,*
Paletto Pubico was born into a rural community from where he gained his love of nature.
His acclaimed work, ***"Feather to Fur"***, has been shown in many of the world's leading galleries.

ABOUT THE AUTHOR

Ken Kennett is an Australian Theatre identity.

He was a foundation actor of the Queensland Theatre Company
and the founder of the Fame Talent Agency and Theatre Company.

In addition, he directed the Westfield Super Juniors for both their stage and television appearances.
Ken was a 2012 recipient of the Order of Australia Medal for his contribution to theatre,
as an Actor, Director and Writer.

ABOUT THE ARTIST

Gérard Maillé is originally from the city of Sète in the south of France.
He studied art at the "Académie des Beaux Arts", and has since developed a repertoire of artistic forms
including paintings, murals and "trompe l'oeil".

As an illustrator, he specialises in character design, caricature and cartooning.

www.ingramcontent.com/pod-product-compliance
Lightning Source LLC
Chambersburg PA
CBHW041428090426
42741CB00002B/75

9780994226402